YOUR'S LOVEABLE DAUGHTER

ROHITA SELLAPAN

Contents

Foreword

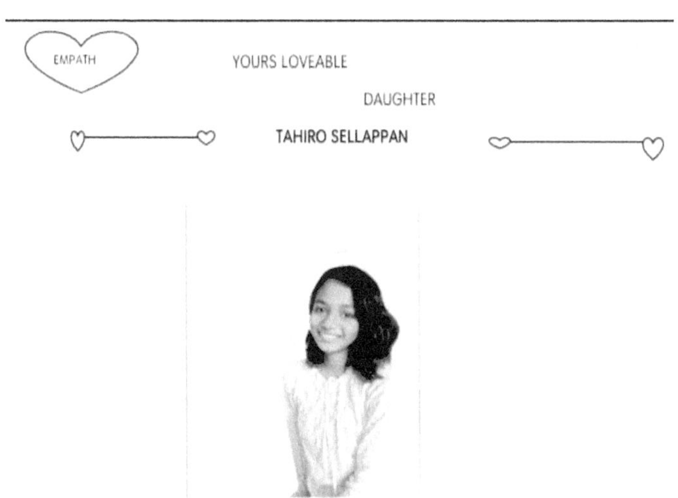

AUTHOR'S NAME: TAHIRO SELLAPPAN
PUBLISHED IN 2022 BY EMPATH PUBLICATION
First edition May 2022

About: Motivation

Acknowledgements

- I would like to express my heartfelt thanks you my parents for their encouragement, hope in me, who has been my moral support at every stage of this book. I am forever indebted to my grandparents who have always motivate me. Their enormous blessings make every life pages of my like more happiness.

- I would like to thank my online teachers from U&I class, who they are taught me English grammar and they have been most patient with me.

I thank all those who have any impact direct or indirect in the making of this book.

Prologue

CONTENT

CHAPTER ONE

YOUR'S LOVEABLE DAUGHTER

YEAR: 2040 (Present day) Reporters meet Tahiro and talk about her. She is chief minister of this state. She is also known as loveable daughter. One of the journalists askTahiro "What inspiring moment that make you to be a chief minister?" She replied "I didn't see my father face, after my father death we don't have enough money. My mother didn't have money to buy amilk to me. At that time no one help us even government, family, friends. My father is a government employee, after his death the government didn't give his pension. They ask bribe. We gave a complain to the head officers, but they also not ready to help us, because of corruption and discrimination. Sometimes we didn't eat anything. This made me to be in this position. I want to help those people who are all surfed like us. I want to change this state from patriarchy,Corruption, discrimination, slavery and murders."

All the journalists got goosebumps of her brave speech.

Writer ROHITA writes TAHIRO's full biographyas a book.

Book name: YOUR'S LOVEABLE DAUGHTER.
YOUR's LOVEABLE DAUGHTERYear: 2007

A new loveable baby girl was born. Her name is Tahiro. But, no one know she become a chief minister. She belongs to a middle class family. She live with her mom and dad. They live a happy life. They Two months later Tahiro's father was death causes of heart attack. After the death of her father she suffered a lot along with her mother. No one isready to help them. After the sudden death of her father. It's become very hard for them to eat foods. There is no enough money to them to lead a good life and to fulfill their basic needs. Tahiro's mother is a brave woman. So, she managed the situation. Tahiro's mother becomes a teacher but she did have money so started tuition in her home. She saves some money for Tahiro education. Years passed, Now Tahiro age is 8. She is a brilliant and Courage girl. She didn't cry at any situation she is emotionally strong. Tahiro and her mother live in small house with large happiness. Tahiro always got 1st prize in speech competition. Her mother always motivates her but she didn't give advice or sermon but by talking and discussing them. Mother said to Tahiro "Not to say lie, be honest, don't break the promise and have courage." When her mother said no one helps us, government didn't give dad's pension money because of bribe, like me more women didn't get their money because of corruption. Tahiro Vow to herself she wants become a loyal chief minister and helps more people like this. Years passed Tahiro age is 18. She is taking her first step as a ward councillor. Once she became a ward councillor. Step by step she is winning in her carrier. She gets energy from her mother. Her mother is a back bone of Tahiro. She is a strict and attitude woman. Tahiro used to work hard and give inspiring speech to people. She work hard but she faced only failure. She took several attempts for her success. She never lost her hope, trust and confident. At the same time her enemy trying to kill her. Her enemy name is Suresh jee, he planned to murder Tahiro. But she is not dead. She didn't take rest even in a critical situation. 2days later, she goesto assembly, she gave a speech but No one hear and listen her speech because she is a women she become angry and she said "you are all must listen my speech". Some Ministers become angry and said "after all you are a woman, men we want to hear yourspeech? It's impossible! We won't listen to you under any circumstances." Tahiro became very angry and said "I will stop your patriarchy" A minister in the crowd beat her. Then she was expelled in the assembly. She left furiously. But she is not crying in that situation. The reason for thetrouble is because she is a woman. At the same time Tahiro hear a bad news. "Her mom is dead". She is not believeshe break downand cries. She goes to the hospital and the doctor said "your mother dead, she took a suicide attempt." But Tahiro does not believe this, because her mother is a brave woman. After she went her house again she worried a lot about her mother, her friends are come to her house. Tahiro said "Without mom there is no world, and without mom there are no words, no love and no money nothing. Her friend's advice she gone, you quickly forget her and achive your aim and don't forget this, and in this state you have more mothers. And we all here for you, and you have your loveable people. At the time some people passing bad comments about her. They spread a news like she is the one who killed her mother. But she didn't hear what they saying.

After she think who was admin my mother in hospital? She started to enquire about this in the hospital, they said "someone called us on the phone and then we went and picked up your mother." Tahiro ask about you give that phone numbers. The Staff give that numbers. She call that number, one of the person took that call and he "your mother was dizzy down in the factory I don't know what happen to her then I call ambulance and admin your mother that's all I know about your mother." Tahiro didn't have to food and slept for past two days but she never lost her confident. Next day Tahiro went to the public meeting. Suresh jee arranged some fake people to make quarrel between Tahiro and people. Tahiro speak to people about what they need for the daily life? But Suresh jee's assistant ask unwanted question to Tahiro that "I'm not saying this is what people are saying. People are saying that you killed your mother. This is true?" Tahiro said "I know I'm not kill my mother and I don't need to prove anyone and my people know about me.Tahiro said to him "My people know that those who are active in justice and virtuous in like will not do an act like this and I do not need to make you understand." People are getting Goosebumps her curious speech. After she finished her speech she meet Suresh jee's assistant and she said "I know who you are. I know what is your intenson is?" But he remains silent and struggle to reply. But they not revealed the truth. Election willcome within three month. Despite a lot of tragedy inside she didn't show it on the outside. She thinks of her countrymore than she think of her mother so long. She going to election campaign and she announced more use full facilities and new act forgeneral people. Tonight before go to sleep she looks her mother photo. Tahiro's car driver see that and he scared to tell the truth to Tahiro. She said "you are the person who can help me to find what happened to my mother, so please help me". At last he said "I was the last one to take your mother in the temple but I didn't pick your mother when she left the temple. She was driving the car." Why my mom could that? Tahiro ask to driver. He said "Your mother followed Suresh jee's car, that's all I know about your mom". She go sleep, with some confident, because she got a clue about her mother's death. Next day, she going to meet Suresh jee's home she asked to him "what happen to my mom? How she died?" He replied "I don't know". "You are the person who killed your mother". He said, First answer my question. But he did not tell the truth and again and again lying. So Tahiro got furious and she came out from his home. Tonight in her dream her mother came and said to her that "Go and see where I was last, don't worrying about me I'm not leave you, I'm always with you, like your shadow, where ever you are I guide you right from wrong and last have courage, be kind and honest always loyal to your people. The next day morning Tahiro remember her dream what her mother said that "go and see where I was last". She goes to meet her mother's car driver. She asked him,"do you know that where is my mom was last you seen?", "I think your mother at last in that old factory" he said. And now we go the place now. They go to the old factory. Tahiro search all places but there is no positive evidence. She isn't Lose her hope for searching there. She search again all place for one proof perhaps there is no evidence. She got upset and she sit down in the floor. Yesterday, she sends a letter to court against Sureshjee about her mother's death. So, she want give any evidence against him. If she doesn't have any evidence against him, she will go to prison. Her mother's car driver said that "mam, I think there is no evidence, so we leave this place. No, said Tahiro that's impossible! We want to search this place once again. So they search again and she stared searching again, and on the time she thought herself "she will not go to prison and how could her mother death". Those things are one cell phone, 2 injections, poison bottle and her mother's bangle. She took that things and bangle and phone is belongs to her mother. Suddenly one of person hit her, she don't know why he hit her. And, he took a gun to shoot her. Suddenly one new person entre into this place and he is Sabari. He saved her life, and she thanks to him. "Are you ok now Tahiro? And Why He trying to shoot you" asks sabari Yeah! I'm fine, I don't know sabari, and this is my destiny. What are you doing here? Sabari asks to Tahiro. She tells all everything to him. Suddenly, he took a gun and he shoots Tahiro. And her car driver come and took her and he admit in hospital. She got unconscious now. She opens her eyes two days after. She saw her friends around her. Tahiro are you alright? Ask her friends. Suddenly she gets out from the hospital, her friends are trying to stop her but she didn't hear their words, and she see her mother's phone for any evidence but her bad time phone isn't operate so she give her mother's phone to the shop. Still these few days for election, so she goes to election campaign. This time people are all surprised and shocked because of her adorable speech. She said to people that "I promise you I will never marriage for you, I am not tell this you for my votes, I trust you that you are all not leave me and we are all forever together". After her campaign she bought her mother's phone and she opens one video and she see that video and her motherrecord some videos. She opens that video "Tahiro, today I came to temple at the same time I met Suresh jee get out into that temple when he seen me, he is acting like a kind man, but I am not believe him, so I'm not fall into his fake words and I thought any strange thing happen today so I follow the Suresh jee's car, suddenly he stopped his car in factory and he go to meet a rowdy to kill Ramesh. He is an honest IAS who against Suresh jee's plan so he plans to kill him." 'Suddenly she put the phone in table that visible to see what is happening. One of the rowdy see her and tell to Suresh jee. He orders to kill her. So he took a gun to kill her. He shoots her, she is dead so Suresh jee put the poison injection to her. 'Bye, bye old lady' said Suresh jee. At last she is died. And he order to call ambulance because he want to show as a good man to people. Ambulance came to the spot and they took her to the hospital. People are all surrounded the place so Suresh jee acting'. After Tahiro see this she dizzy down and her friends took to hospital. After some hour she opens her eyes she ask to her friends that where is my phone and other evidence. They took that all, after she this evidence, she is peace in mind. Tomorrow is election and last day to proceeding evidence against Suresh jee. Suresh jee's agent in hospital his name in Kavin. Tahiro's friends are standing outside to safe her. Suresh jee's agent works as doctor in his hospital. When Tahiro is dizzy, he stolen her phone and place a fake phone she give to Suresh jee. Next Tahiro and Suresh jee are assemble in court and Tahiro see Sabari near Suresh jee. Then she understand why he shoots her because he gets money to Suresh jee to kill her. She realize that her mother's phone was stolen by Suresh jee's agent. At the timeelection result will announced. Tahiro's heart beating very fact because of her evidence was stolen. Suresh jee isn't afraid. The judge came. Judge is started to speak. He asked to Tahirothat "Ms. Tahiro you have any evidence against Suresh jee?" She didn't speakfew minutes and she said "YES". Suresh jee is shocked and said "that's impossible it will not happen she is lying". How Mr. Suresh jee? You said confidently. He silently sat in his place. Tahiro proceeding her evidence bangle, injection and cell phone. Suresh jee isn't afraid because this is a fake phone. When Judge is turn on the cell phone but it is not turn on. Suresh jee is said "Sir I already said you I am not kill her mother, she is the only girl who kill her mother, people are found she killed her mother so she don't complained me and, it is a fake cell phone". "This is my time Mr. Suresh jee. So you keep quiet and sit down" said Tahiro. "Oh! Said Suresh jee Yes, I know this is your time, so show the exact evidence that what it means is that you killed your mother." If a lie is told over and over again it will not be true. I know I am not killed my mother, It's not necessary to prove to you. Ok, said Suresh jee then show your evidence. "I know Mr. Suresh jee don't order me" said Tahiro angrily. "Order! Order! Order! Calm and sit down this is Court not your assembly" said judge. Again judge is turn on the phone but phone is not open. And she calls her friend Kaviya who was a white hacker. She came and checks the cell phone and cell phone is opened Tahiro's mother cell phone. Suresh jee is not shocked because he knew that there is not video about him. After turn on her cell phone she shows that Suresh jee killed her mother and he know about Ramesh IAS video. The judge saw all evidence against Suresh jee. How he saw this evidence means

Kavin isn't Suresh jee's agent he is Tahiro's agent he give to Suresh jee to fake cell phone. For all the mistakes and he made to kill the judge give impunity to Suresh jee death, penalty for his more murders. And Tahiro go to election result place. Her ministers believe her because she is a woman, so they are not responding to Tahiro's word. They are all thought that she is not winning this election, she lied to their thinking. At last she won this battle. After she won this battle her ministers are all give response to her but they are acting. Wow! Said Tahiro I want to learn something from you which I say is that i have to learn how to act from you. Don't judge a woman is silent. She does her work honestly. Sometime Tahiro think of her mother and her quote that "don't talk lie, don't break the promise, be honest and have Courage". Tahiro honestly rule her state in a good way. People are happy for her judgments. And she thinks 10years of her struggles. When she won this battle after 10 years, she felt very proud about herself. She saved her promise, which once she said

election camping is not married across the life.

Do you know the name of Tahiro's mother?

Your mother's name is also Tahiro's mother's name.

What is clearly from this everyone, who made mistakes they will surly get punish.

Mother is Back bone of every living being. So respect your mother's words.

There is a woman behind everysuccess and she is the mother.

A BRAVE SOLDIER

It is the village name DOLAKSAR. Anandhiraviyan is living in this village. He is 24 years old. He is such a brilliant boy but he isn't brave, he didn't talk anyone because they are always discouraging him for his afraid. His dad is a police so, he want to his son also become a police but Anandhiraviyan dislike that so his dad also discourage him. Next day, he and his family go to temple. The Temple celebrates the ceremony in 12 years once; many army soldiers are vigilance around the temple. Anandhiraviyangoing top of the temple and he saw a toy gun so he took that, and cipher to one of the soldiers he accidentally press the shoot point, but this is a real gun, and all the soldiers are look him and he is scared dizzy down. After sometime he opens his eyes. Soldiers are ready to shoot him. He so scared of them and he tell the truth. They not considered. They give two opportunities to him (1st He goes to jail & 2nd He wants to join the army soldier). When hear the 2nd one, he started to cry, he accepted 1st.But his parents forced him to join Army. He went be join A NEW SOLDIER. Soldiers give practice to Anandhiraviyan to become a soldier.He goes to his 1st mission at Jammu and Kashmiri. He isn't shooting anyone else he goes to hide himself. All the soldiers are angry to him, because he didn't shoot anyone. His head officer meet him and said "you can do anything, you are so brave and knowledgeable person Anandhiraviyan, so you don't afraid to anything you can do anything" said the head officer. His 2nd mission he do his best, he didn't afraid to shoot anyone. ALL the soldiers are surprised his brave. And joint army soldier permanently in*A BRAVE SOLDIER.....*

MORAL: DO NOT BLAM OTHERS EVEN IF THEY MAKE MISTAKES.... ENCOURAGE OTHER

LAWS OF LIFE

- EDUCATION is just not a word

  This is a bullet, which shoot your enemies.

- PARENTS is just not a word

  This is a fake mirror, which you show hate them but they reflect you love.

- FRIENDSHIP is just not a word

  This is a precious thing, which didn't have any secrets.

- UNIVERSAL {god} is just not a word

  This is a soul, which gives us hope.

- EGO is just not a word

  This is devil, which kills your happiness.
  MONEY is just not a word
  This is a paper, which gives you fake people.
  *LIVE HAPPY LIFE AND HAVE FUN WITHOUT DISCRIMINATION.
  *DON'T THINK ANYTHINK DEEPLY THAT KILLS YOUR HAPPINESS.
  *ACHIEVEMENT AND WINNING IS MOST POWERFULL WEAPONS TO YOUR ENEMY AND ENVIOUS PEOPLE.
  *NEVER EVER STOP YOUR HARD WORK, ANYTIME IT WILL HELP YOU.
  *TIME AND AGE NEVER WAIT FOR ANYONE.

*EDUCATION IS A KEY TO OPEN YOUR HAPPY AND BEAUTIFUL LIFE.

*WHEN YOU FEEL "YOU DON'T HAVE ANYTHING" YOU THINK THE GREAT 2PERSONS, WHICH THEY HADN'T ANY SOURCE IN THEIR CHILDHOOD.

1. A.P.J. ABDUL KALAM
2. ABRAHAM LINCOLN.

*THE PERSON WHO WAS DEPRESSED TOO, THINKS YOUR CHILDHOOD MEMORIES (OR) SEES YOUR CHILDHOOD PHOTOS.

*WHEN A MAN HAS AN OLD IDEA HE WILL NEVER THINK OF A NEW IDEA.

*MAKE YOU ALWAYS BUSY.

*WHAT YOU WANT THAT DEFENATLY NOT HAPPEN, WHAT YOU NEED THAT DEFENATLY HAPPEN.

*DO YOUR THINGS UNIQUE, MAKE SOMETHING POSSIBLE.

*Money isn't your destination, it's your freaking desire.

Don't believe hard work

Don't believe hard work because once my senior said me that she prepare for her JEE exam and she almost cover all the lessons, her exam was came, when she saw her question paper she became very happy but she isn't score more marks and she didn't pass the exam too, in that exam because she didn't have much time to complete the answers. Her 2nd attempt she didn't work hard for her study, but she score more marks! Because she gave first priority to high mark questions, and next she wrote what she know. HERE, the Hard work isn't work for winning but Smart work done. Iam not against to hard work you do your work happily and smartly, you will win the world easily. In this, we learn two things:1. Time is precious 2. Smart work

Hard work beats Smart work

SUCCESSFUL LIFE

FIRST MAKE YOUR CLEAR PLAN FOR YOUR DECISION AND YOU STATED TO RUN, ONCE YOU ENTRED INTO THE RACE DON'T EXPECT ANYTHING AND ANYONE. DON'T BELIEVE WHAT YOU HEAR. MIDDLE OF RACE YOU TAKE REST. IF YOU LOSS OR WIN, YOU CONTINUE THE RACE UNTILL YOU WIN THE LIFE.